MONEY
Doesn't Grow on Trees

By Julie Ellis

Contents

Money Doesn't Grow on Trees! 2

Rule 1: Set Money Goals 4

Rule 2: Earn Money 8

Rule 3: Start Saving 14

Rule 4: Make a Budget 16

Rule 5: Be a Smart Spender 20

Glossary 24

Money Doesn't Grow on Trees!

Have you ever heard an adult say, "Money doesn't grow on trees"? What they really mean is that money is not easy to get. Money doesn't just sprout up out of the ground, or bloom on a branch for you to pick.

Have you ever thought, "When I grow up, I want to be rich"? If money doesn't grow on trees, then how can you ever become rich?

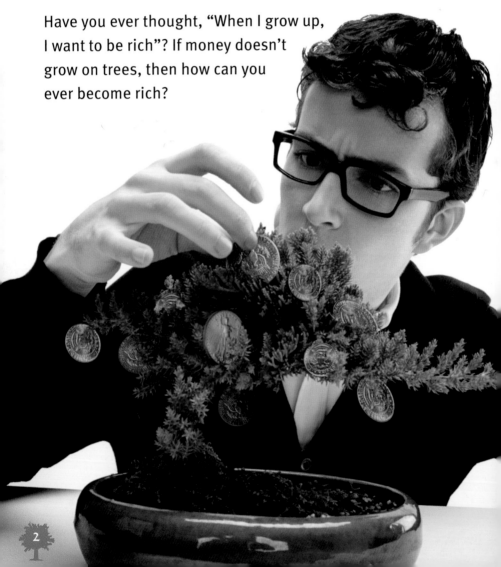

Get-Rich Method 1: Win the Lottery

It is true that, if you won the **lottery,** you'd get a lot of money. But you can't count on winning the lottery. You have a much better chance of being struck by lightning than winning the lottery. It is not a smart way to try to get rich.

Get-Rich Method 2: Follow Five Simple Money Rules

- Rule 1: Set Money Goals

- Rule 2: Earn Money

- Rule 3: Start Saving

- Rule 4: Make a **Budget**

- Rule 5: Be a Smart Spender

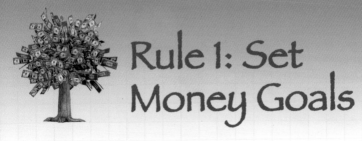

Rule 1: Set Money Goals

Think of a **money goal** as a target. Set a target for something that you want to buy or spend your money on, so you have something to aim for. If your goal is something you need money for quickly, like going to the movies, it is a short-term goal. If it is something big for your future, like a bike, it is a long-term goal.

Money goals:

- help you avoid wasting your money on bad choices
- help you become good at saving for things
- help you buy only what you want or need
- give you a reason to work hard when you don't feel like working.

Thinking about a Money Goal

1. Do you know the **value** of each coin and bill?
2. Can you give the correct amount of money, or check that you receive the right amount of change, when you buy something?
3. What one item would you buy if you had a lot of money right now? How much would it cost?
4. How much money would you like to spend or save each week?
5. What can you do to earn money?
6. How much money could you earn in one week?

Have you ever broken something and then had to pay to have it fixed? Malik broke his family's TV screen playing soccer inside. His parents said he had to pay $100 toward the cost of a new TV. There was a soccer game Malik wanted to watch on TV in four weeks. So Malik wanted to pay off the $100 **debt** he owed his parents as soon as he could.

Malik had $11.00 saved, so he needed to earn the rest. On Saturday, he held a car wash. He charged $5.00 for each wash and washed five cars. Over the next four weeks, Malik emptied the dishwasher for $7.00 each week. He also walked the neighbor's dog four days a week for four weeks. They paid him $3.00 per walk.

1. What was Malik's goal?

2. What plans did Malik make to reach his goal?

3. Did Malik reach his goal?

Answers on page 23

How to Set a Money Goal

Step 1: Decide what you want to spend your money on, for example, a bike, or a trip to an amusement park.

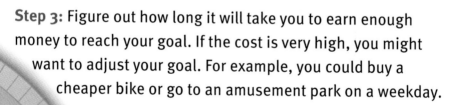

Step 2: Figure out how much money your goal costs. Be sure to plan for extra costs. They add up quickly. For example, if you buy a bike, you will need to buy a helmet, too. If you go to an amusement park, you will probably need money for food while you are there.

Step 3: Figure out how long it will take you to earn enough money to reach your goal. If the cost is very high, you might want to adjust your goal. For example, you could buy a cheaper bike or go to an amusement park on a weekday.

Step 4: Ask your parents or caregiver if it's all right for you to work toward this goal.

Step 5: Find a job that suits you. Then start working and saving your money.

Step 6: Write down your money goal in a notebook. Add pictures of your goal to the notebook. Make sure you look at it every day to remind yourself why you are working so hard.

Rule 2: Earn Money

Earning money is very important if you want to meet your money goal. Earning money means you can:

- buy things you need
- buy things you want
- save money for the future
- learn how to divide up your money into saving, spending, and sharing groups.

The Do's of Earning Money

1. Do ask your parents or caregiver if it's okay for you to get a job.

2. Do make sure you get your homework and regular chores done in addition to earning money.

3. Do have a safe place to keep your earnings.

The Don'ts of Earning Money

1. Don't ask strangers for work.

2. Don't give out personal details (like putting your home phone number on any **advertisements**).

3. Don't take on more jobs than you can handle.

Ten Ideas to Earn Money

1. Animal caregiver – walk dogs, brush cats, feed pets, clean out cages or fish tanks.

2. Out-of-the-house jobs – babysit, deliver newspapers, wash cars, wash windows, run errands.

3. Gardening – rake leaves, pull weeds, mow lawns.

4. Bake sale – bake cakes, cookies, muffins, cupcakes.

5. Crafts – make and sell bird feeders, jewelry, holiday cards.

6. Seasonal jobs – wrap gifts, shovel snow, sell fresh fruits and vegetables, sell lemonade.

7. Family help – unpack groceries, make meals, entertain a younger sibling, do housework.

8. Rental library – have friends pay to **borrow** your books, video games, or toys.

9. Yard sale – sell your old toys, clothes, books.

10. Teaching a skill or tutoring – teach older relatives or neighbors to use e-mail, help younger kids with their homework.

Follow the flowchart below to find the best job for you.

START

Do you like animals?

✔ Yes → **Animal caregiver**

✗ No → **Do you like making things?**

Do you like making things?

✗ No → **Do you like to be active?**

✔ Yes → **Make and sell crafts**

Do you like to be active?

✔ Yes → **Out-of-the-house jobs**

✗ No → **Do you like growing things?**

Do you like growing things?

✗ No → **Out-of-the-house jobs**

✔ Yes → **Gardening or seasonal jobs**

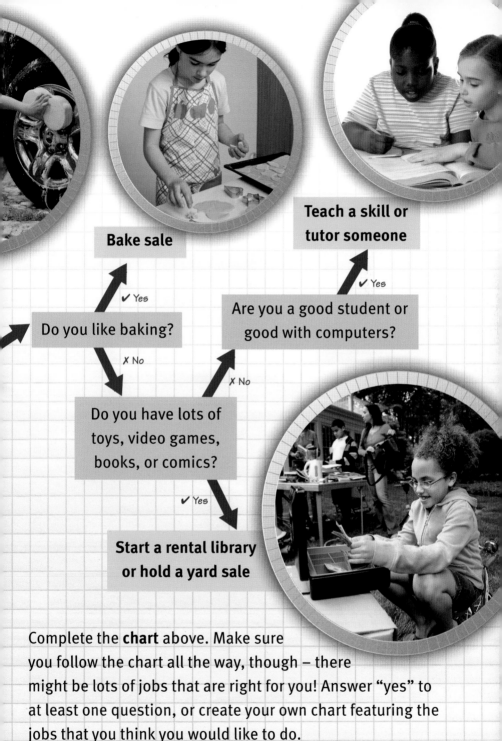

Bake sale

Teach a skill or tutor someone

✔ Yes

Do you like baking?

Are you a good student or good with computers?

✔ Yes

✘ No

✘ No

Do you have lots of toys, video games, books, or comics?

✔ Yes

Start a rental library or hold a yard sale

Complete the **chart** above. Make sure you follow the chart all the way, though – there might be lots of jobs that are right for you! Answer "yes" to at least one question, or create your own chart featuring the jobs that you think you would like to do.

Ruby the Lawn Mower

Ruby was strong and enjoyed helping people. She played on the school basketball team, and she needed a way to stay in shape over the summer. One day, she helped her mother mow the lawn. Ruby did such a good job that she thought she'd do the same thing for others around the neighborhood.

Ruby made a flier advertising her services. She gave copies of the flier to friends and neighbors. In eight weeks, she got eleven jobs. It took her two hours to cut each lawn.

How much money did Ruby earn in eight weeks?

Summer Is Coming!
Do you need your lawn mowed?

A reliable, careful, and efficient lawn mower is available to keep your yard looking its best!

E-mail Ruby at beautiful_lawn@e-mail.com

$5.00 per hour

Answers on page 23

Rule 3: Start Saving

All of the money you receive is called **income**. Allowance money, gift money, and the money you earn are all income. The part of your income that you don't spend is called **savings**.

If you want to buy something that costs more money than you have, you will need to save your money.

Savings		Earnings		New game
$20.00	+	$30.00	=	$50.00

The less money you earn, the more important it is for you to save. If you save a little money each week, one day you will have a lot of money.

Save		in 1 year		Saved in 1 year
$2.00 per week	×	52 weeks	=	$104.00

Mei and her two friends want to see a movie. Mei's father says it will be cheaper to rent a movie to watch at home. How much money would Mei and her friends save if they rented a movie instead of going out to the movies?

The movies		Rented movie	
3 movie tickets	$24.00	1 rented movie	$4.00
popcorn for 3 at the movies	$12.00	popcorn for 3 at home	$2.00
drinks for 3 at the movies	$9.00	drinks for 3 at home	$4.00

Answers on page 23

Rule 4: Make a Budget

You have set a money goal, earned enough money, and purchased what you wanted. Now what? Do you give up your job because you don't need it any longer, or do you keep working and buy something you don't really want just because you can? A better idea is to keep working and saving instead. Even if you don't have a new money goal, you will need to make a budget so you don't waste the money you earn. A budget is a plan for saving and spending money. It helps you keep track of the money you have coming in. It shows your earnings or allowance, as well as the money you have going out, including spending, saving, and sharing money.

A Three-Jar Budget

A simple way to budget is the three-jar method. Get three jars and label them "Save," "Spend," and "Share." Put some of your money in each jar.

Emilio is 11. He gets a $6.00 allowance each week. Emilio puts $3.00 in his save jar and $2.00 in his spend jar. He puts the rest of his money in a share jar. He plans to donate the share jar to a **charity** once it's full. How much will Emilio be able to share after 20 weeks?

Answers on page 23

A Notebook Budget

A notebook is a quick way to record your budget. It is an easy way to see how much you are earning, saving, and spending.

Ella is 10. She can earn up to $20.00 a week working around her neighborhood. She keeps a record of what she has earned, spent, and saved. How much did she save last week?

	Money Earned	Money Spent	Money Saved
Monday	Do laundry $2		$2
Tuesday	Rake leaves $5		$5
Wednesday		Candy bar $1	−$1
Thursday	Load and empty dishwasher $1		$1
Friday		Movies $12	−$12
Saturday	Wash car $6		$6
Sunday	Sweep garage $3		$3
TOTAL	$17	$13	?

Answers on page 23

A Spreadsheet Budget

If you like using the computer, you could keep your earnings on a computer **spreadsheet**. You can ask an adult to help you set one up, or download one already made from the Internet.

Nadia is 12. She has two goals. She is saving for a **secondhand** snowboard, and to buy a car when she is old enough. Nadia earns $20 a week working as an animal caregiver. She does a monthly spreadsheet budget. How much did she save in May? How much has she saved by the end of June?

Nadia's Budget				
	Money Earned	**Money Spent**	**Money Saved**	**Running total saved**
April	$80	$15 Food	$65	$65
May	$80	$20 Book	?	$125
June	$80	$12 Movies	$68	?

Answers on page 23

19

Rule 5: Be a Smart Spender

Smart spenders are people who get the best value for their money. They compare prices before they buy something. They keep a budget, so they know exactly how much money they are earning, saving, and spending. They know exactly how much money they have at any moment.

If you are a smart spender, you will:

- make your hard-earned money go farther
- reach your money goals faster
- save more money for the future.

It's not difficult to be a smart spender. Here are some ways you can become one:

- Compare the price of the same item sold in different places
- Buy secondhand items
- Buy items you need when they're **discounted** or on sale
- Find cheaper ways to do things; for example, rent a DVD rather than buy it
- Always save some money before you spend any money
- Be aware of hidden costs like **shipping and handling** costs
- Write down your earnings, savings, and spending.

Nicholas got $25.00 for his birthday. He wants to buy a new video game. He can buy it at the electronics store for $22.00. He can buy it on the Internet for $18.00, plus $5.00 shipping and handling. He can buy it from the secondhand game store for $13.00. He can also borrow it for free from the library, but there is a three-week waiting list.

What should Nicholas do?

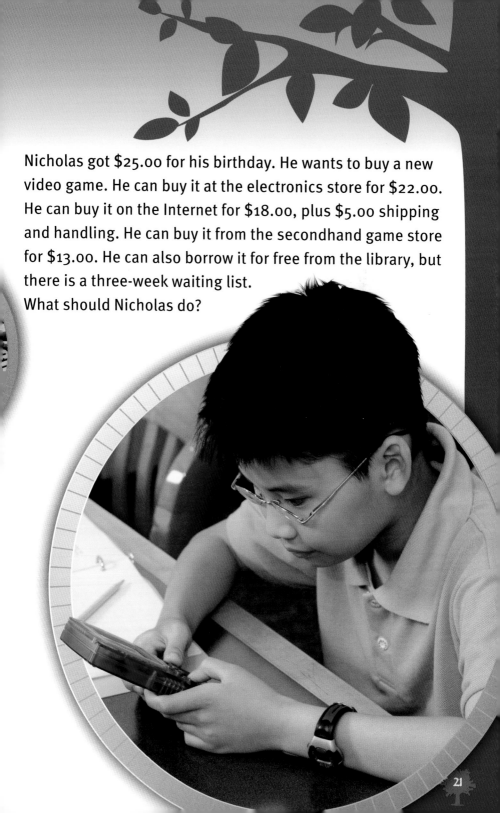

By now, chances are you aren't planning to get rich by winning the lottery. It's almost certain that you won't get rich by winning your money. Yet if you work hard and follow the five simple rules in this book, you have every chance in the world to set up a wonderful future for yourself.

The next time someone says to you, "Money doesn't grow on trees," you can be sure they are telling the truth. Perhaps then you can let them in on the real secrets to getting rich!

Answers:

1. Malik's goal was to earn $89 within four weeks (he had $11 saved).

2. Malik planned to have a car wash, empty the dishwasher, and walk the neighbor's dog.

3. Yes, Malik earned $101 in four weeks
   (5 x $5.00) + (4 x $7.00) + (16 x $3.00) = $101.00.

Ruby earned $110 in 8 weeks (11 jobs x 2 hours = 22 hours; 22 hours x $5.00 = $110.00).

Mei and her friends would have spent $45.00 to go to the movies. They would have spent $10.00 for a rented movie and snacks at home. By choosing the rented movie, they would save $35.00 ($45.00 − $10.00 = $35.00).

Emilio will be able to share $20.00 after 20 weeks ($1.00 saved x 20 weeks = $20.00).

Ella saved $4.00 ($17.00 earned − $13.00 spent = $4.00 saved).

Nadia saved $60.00 in May ($80.00 earned − $20.00 spent = $60.00 saved). Nadia had saved $193 by the end of June ($125.00 running total + $68.00 saved = $193.00).

Glossary

advertisements[1] – signs or recordings telling others about a service you can offer

borrow[4] – to use something for a while and promise to return it later

budget – a plan for saving and spending money

charity – an organization that helps people in need

chart[1] – a visual display of information

debt[7] – money that you owe to someone else

discounted – offered at a special price, cheaper than the normal price

earning[4] – making money by working

income[4] – all the money you get

lottery – a game of chance where people buy tickets with numbers on them and the winner is chosen randomly

money goal – a target amount you want to save

savings[4] – the part of your income you don't spend or share

secondhand – when something has been owned and used by someone else

shipping and handling – the extra money you pay when an item is shipped to you

spreadsheet – a computer program that can be used to create tables and charts

value[4] – the amount of money considered to be a fair price for something

Academic Vocabulary Key		4	Economics	8	US History	12	Technology
1	English Language Arts	5	Civics	9	World History	13	General Arts
2	Mathematics	6	Geography	10	Health	14	Dance/Music
3	Science	7	General History	11	Physical Education	15	Theater/Visual Arts